Light tomorrow with today!

—ELIZABETH BARRETT BROWNING (1806-1851)
English poet

A WOMAN'S JOURNAL

Life begets life. Energy creates energy.
It is by spending oneself that one becomes rich.

—SARAH BERNHARDT (1844-1923)
French actress

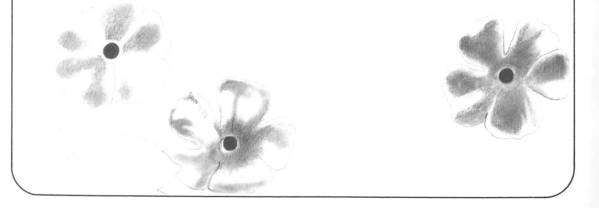

Good communication is as stimulating as black coffee,
and just as hard to sleep after.

—ANNE MORROW LINDBERGH, b. 1906
American writer & aviator

Advice is what we ask for when we already know the answer but wish we didn't.

—ERICA JONG, b. 1942
American writer

Joy is a net of love by which you can catch souls.

—MOTHER TERESA, b. 1910
Roman Catholic Missionary

We don't see things as they are, we see things as we are.

—ANAÏS NIN (1903-1977)
American/French writer

I have enough for this life. If there is no other life, then this one has been enough to make it worth being born, myself a human being.

—PEARL S. BUCK (1892-1973)
American writer & humanitarian

A woman's life can really be a succession of lives, each revolving around some emotionally compelling situation or challenge, and each marked off by some intense experience.

—WALLIS SIMPSON, DUCHESS OF WINDSOR (1896-1986)

One is not born a woman, one becomes one.

—SIMONE DE BEAUVOIR (1908–1986)
French writer & philosopher

I am never afraid of what I know.

—ANNA SEWELL (1820-1878)
English writer

*She must not swing her arms as though they were dangling ropes, she must
not switch herself this way and that; she must not shout and she must not,
while wearing her bridal veil, smoke a cigarette.*

—EMILY POST (1873-1960)
American hostess & writer

It's the good girls who keep the diaries; the bad girls never have the time.

—TALLULAH BANKHEAD (1903-1968)
American actress

Only friends will tell you the truths you need to hear to make the last part of your life bearable.

—FRANCINE DU PLESSIX GRAY, b. 1930
French writer

Personally, I think if a woman hasn't met the right man by the time she's 24,
she may be lucky.

—DEBORAH KERR, b. 1921
Scottish actress

There was a definite process by which one made people into friends, and it involved talking to them and listening to them for hours at a time.

—REBECCA WEST (1892-1983)
English writer

One can never consent to creep when one feels an impulse to soar.

—HELEN KELLER (1880-1968)
American writer

The most popular labor-saving device is still money.

—PHYLLIS GEORGE, b. 1949
American sports broadcaster

But what are we but our bad habits? They make us feel alive, don't they?

—MARILYN HARRIS
20th-century American writer

If only one could tell true love from false love as one can tell mushrooms from toadstools.

—KATHERINE MANSFIELD (1888–1923)
New Zealand writer

Eternity is not something that begins after you are dead. It is going on all the time. We are in it now.

—CHARLOTTE PERKINS GILMAN (1860-1935)
American writer

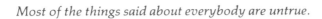

Most of the things said about everybody are untrue.

—EDITH EVANS (1888-1976)
English actress

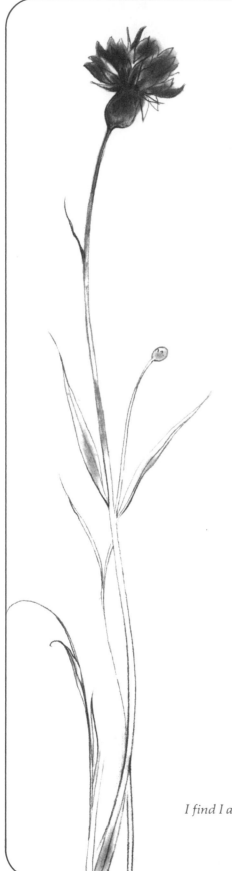

I find I always have to write something *on a steamed mirror.*

—ELAINE DUNDY
20th-century American writer

Fortunately analysis is not the only way to resolve inner conflicts. Life itself still remains a very effective therapist.

—KAREN HORNEY (1885-1952)
American psychoanalyst

The truly free woman is one who knows how to decline a dinner invitation without giving an excuse.

—ANONYMOUS

Brevity is the soul of lingerie.

—DOROTHY PARKER (1893-1967)
American writer

It is far harder to kill a phantom than a reality.

—VIRGINIA WOOLF (1882-1941)
English writer

Avoiding danger is no safer in the long run than outright exposure. The fearful are caught as often as the bold.

—HELEN KELLER (1880-1968)
American writer

*What's terrible is to pretend that the second-rate is first-rate. To pretend
that you don't need love when you do; or you like your work when you
know quite well you're capable of better.*

—DORIS LESSING, b.1919
British writer

You can't fake listening. It shows.

—RAQUEL WELCH, b. 1942
American actress

It makes perfect sense to me that people would want to be married. But for me, security is not knowing what's going to happen. Because if I don't know, it could be terrific.

—GLORIA STEINEM, b. 1934
American feminist & writer

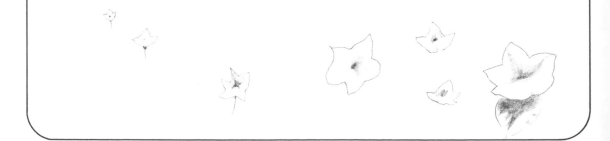

When we can begin to take our failures non-seriously, it means we are ceasing to be afraid of them. It is of immense importance to learn to laugh at ourselves.

—KATHERINE MANSFIELD (1888–1923)
New Zealand writer

Marrying a man is like buying something you've been admiring for a long time in a shop window. You may love it when you get it home, but it doesn't always go with everything else.

—JEAN KERR, b. 1923
American playwright & humorist

Living never wore one out so much as the effort not to live.

—ANAÏS NIN (1903-1977)
American/French writer

Part of the trouble is that I've never properly understood that some disasters accumulate, that they don't all land like a child out of an apple tree.

—JANET BURROWAY, b. 1937
American writer

I have a woman inside my soul.

—YOKO ONO, b. 1933
Japanese/American singer

What seems like courage is really persistence—the ability to put part of yourself on hold—Patience.

—BARBARA GORDON
20th-century American writer

Life is to be lived. If you have to support yourself, you had bloody well better find some way that is going to be interesting. And you don't do that by sitting around wondering about yourself.

—KATHARINE HEPBURN, b. 1909
American actress

I'm as pure as the driven slush.

—TALLULAH BANKHEAD (1903-1968)
American actress

If only we'd stop trying to be happy, we could have a pretty good time.

—EDITH WHARTON (1862-1937)
American novelist

The best mind-altering drug is truth.

—LILY TOMLIN, b. 1939
American actress & comedienne

Why not seize the pleasure at once? How often is happiness destroyed by preparation, foolish preparation!

—JANE AUSTEN (1775-1817)
English writer

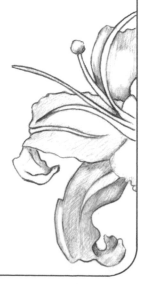

Tears may be dried up, but the heart—never.

—MARGUERITE DE VALOIS (1553-1615)
French princess & scholar

Guilt is the price we pay willingly for doing what we are going to do anyway.

—ISABELLE HOLLAND
20th-century English writer

*What the hell—you might be right, you might
be wrong—but don't just avoid.*

—KATHARINE HEPBURN, b. 1909
American actress

For most of history, Anonymous was a woman.

—VIRGINIA WOOLF (1882-1941)
English writer

For no actual process happens twice; only we meet the same sort of occasion again.

—SUZANNE K. LANGER (1895–1985)
American educator & philosopher

Imagination is the highest kite one can fly.

—LAUREN BACALL, b. 1924
American actress

Strength is the capacity to break a chocolate bar into four pieces with your bare hands—and then eat just one of the pieces.

—JUDITH VIORST, b. 1931
American poet

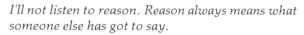

*I'll not listen to reason. Reason always means what
someone else has got to say.*

—ELIZABETH GASKELL (1810-1865)
English writer

A woman must have money and a room of her own.

—VIRGINIA WOOLF (1882-1941)
English writer

Each person has his own safe place—running, painting, swimming, fishing, weaving, gardening. The activity itself is less important than the act of drawing on your own resources.

—BARBARA GORDON
20th-century American writer

The Eskimo has fifty-two names for snow because it is important to them;
there ought to be as many for love.

—MARGARET ATWOOD, b. 1939
Canadian writer

No one worth possessing can be quite possessed.

—SARA TEASDALE (1884-1933)
American poet

If you want a place in the sun, you've got to put up with a few blisters.

—ABIGAIL VAN BUREN, b.1918
American columnist

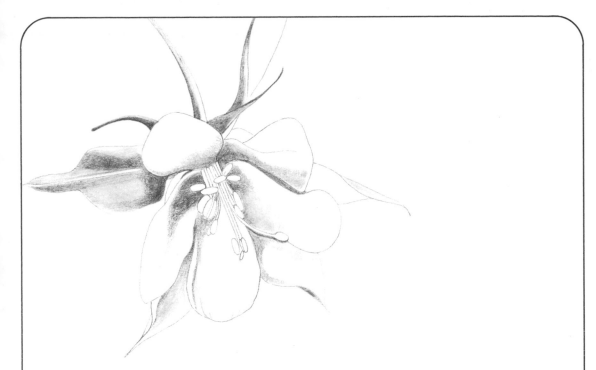

Man forgives woman anything save the wit to outwit him.

—MINNA ANTRIM
19th-century Irish writer

To fall in love is awfully simple, but to fall out of love is simply awful.

—BESS MYERSON, b. 1924
American columnist

You don't know a woman until you have had a letter from her.

—ADA LEVERSON (1862-1933)
English writer

I like living. I have sometimes been wildly, despairingly, acutely miserable, racked with sorrow, but through it all I still know quite certainly that just to be alive is a grand thing.

—AGATHA CHRISTIE (1890-1976)
English writer

Nobody can make you feel inferior without your consent.

—ELEANOR ROOSEVELT (1884-1962)
American stateswoman & humanitarian

One of the things about equality is not just that you be treated equally to a man, but that you treat yourself equally to the way you treat a man.

—MARLO THOMAS, b.1943
American actress

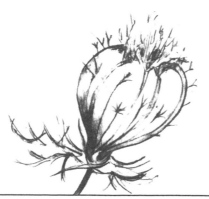

We are always the same age inside.

—GERTRUDE STEIN (1874-1946)
American writer

Fond as we are of our loved ones, there comes at times during their absence an unexplainable peace.

—ANNE SHAW
20th-century American writer

Life is either a daring adventure or nothing.

—HELEN KELLER (1880-1968)
American writer

There are no more thorough prudes than those who have some little secret to hide.

—GEORGE SAND (Amandine-Aurore-Lucile Dupin, 1804-1876)
French writer

I see no reason to keep silent about my enjoyment of the sound of my own voice as I work.

—MURIEL SPARK, b. 1918
Scottish writer

It is better to be looked over than overlooked.

—MAE WEST (1893-1980)
American actress

Man loves little and often; woman much and rarely.

—ANONYMOUS

The trouble with some women is that they get all excited about nothing—and then marry him.

—CHER, b. 1946
American actress

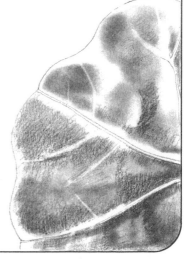

It would be curious to discover who it is to whom one writes in a diary. Possibly to some mysterious personification of one's own identity.

—BEATRICE WEBB (1858-1954)
American sociologist

We are tomorrow's past.

—MARY WEBB (1881-1927)
Scottish writer

If I look fabulous or if I look haggard and awful, it's the lighting . . . my first advice to women concerned about their appearance is to check the lights in their living room.

—BARBARA WALTERS, b. 1931
American journalist

The dream was always running ahead of one. To catch up, to live for a moment in unison with it, that was the miracle.

—ANAÏS NIN (1903-1977)
American/French writer

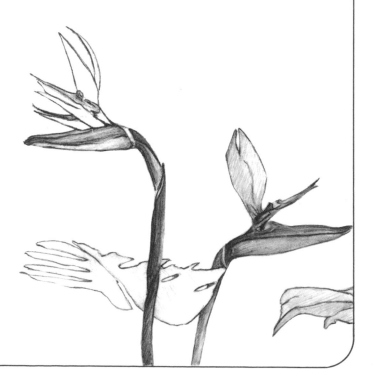

There's nothing half so real in life as the things you've done . . . inexorably,
unalterably done.

—SARA TEASDALE (1884-1933)
American poet

Everything else you grow out of, but you never recover from childhood.

—BERYL BAINBRIDGE, b. 1933
American writer

Sometimes I wonder if men and women really suit each other. Perhaps they should live next door and just visit now and then.

—KATHARINE HEPBURN, b. 1909
American actress

Life is what happens to you when you're making other plans.

—BETTY TALMADGE, b. 1924
American meat broker

It is easy to be independent when you've got money. But to be independent when you haven't got a thing—that's the Lord's test.

—MAHALIA JACKSON (1911-1972)
American gospel singer

To keep our faces toward change and behave like free spirits in the presence of fate is strength undefeatable.

—HELEN KELLER (1880-1968)
American writer

Love never dies of starvation, but often of indigestion.

—NINON DE LENCLOS (1620-1705)
French courtesan

Cleaning your house while your kids are still growing is like shoveling the walk before it stops snowing.

—PHYLLIS DILLER, b. 1917
American comedienne

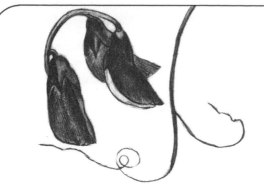

Now I think everyone should ask, "Am I going to be able to be the person I want to be in this relationship?"

—ALI MacGRAW, b. 1939
American actress

At the end, it means more than religion to have had a happy childhood.
Memory of it serves to hold off pain and fear; it is an unfailing resource.

—HELEN HOOVEN SANTMYER
20th-century American writer

I'm just going to write because I cannot help it.

—CHARLOTTE BRONTË (1816–1855)
English writer

Time is a dressmaker specializing in alterations.

—FAITH BALDWIN
20th-century American writer

*Creative minds have always been known to survive
any kind of bad training.*

—ANNA FREUD (1895-1982)
Austrian psychoanalyst

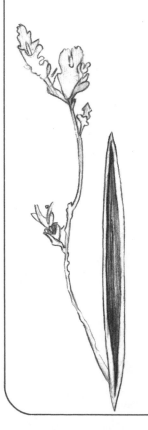

Tact is after all a kind of mindreading.

—SARAH ORNE JEWETT (1849-1909)
American writer

Boyfriends weren't friends at all; they were prizes, escorts, symbols of achievement, fascinating strangers, the Other.

—SUSAN ALLEN TOTH, b. 1940
American writer

If I'm too strong for some people, that's their problem.

—GLENDA JACKSON, b. 1936
English actress

. . . the greater part of our happiness or misery depends on our dispositions and not on our circumstances.

—MARTHA WASHINGTON (1731-1802)
American First Lady

Fate keeps on happening.

—ANITA LOOS (1893-1981)
American writer

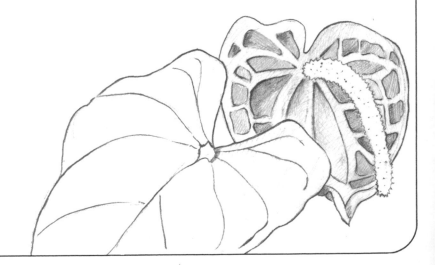

It seems to me we can never give up longing and wishing while we are alive. There are certain things we feel to be beautiful and good, and we must hunger for them.

—GEORGE ELIOT (Mary Ann Evans, 1819-1880)
English writer

We can only learn to love by loving.

—IRIS MURDOCH, b. 1919
Irish writer

Men are taught to apologize for their weaknesses,
women for their strengths.

—LOIS WYSE, b. 1926
American advertising executive

"Stay" is a charming word in a friend's vocabulary.

—LOUISA MAY ALCOTT (1832-1888)
American writer

*I've dreamt in my life dreams that have stayed with me ever after, and
changed my ideas; they've gone through and through me, like wine through
water, and altered the colour of my mind.*

—EMILY BRONTË (1818-1848)
English writer

Gossip is the opiate of the oppressed.

—ERICA JONG, b. 1942
American writer

A broken heart is what makes life so wonderful five years later, when you see the guy in an elevator and he is fat and smoking a cigar and saying long-time-no-see. If he hadn't broken your heart, you couldn't have that glorious feeling of relief!

—PHYLLIS BATELLE, b. 1922
American journalist

In youth we learn; in age we understand.

—MARIE von EBNER-ESCHENBACH (1830-1916)
Austrian writer

All we're ever looking for is another open door.

—KATE BUSH, b. 1958
English singer/songwriter

If truth is beauty, how come no one has their hair done in a library?

—LILY TOMLIN, b. 1939
American actress & comedienne

I like people who refuse to speak until they are ready to speak.

—LILLIAN HELLMAN (1907-1984)
American writer

*Romance and work are great diversions to keep you
from dealing with yourself.*

—CHER, b. 1946
American actress

We all live with the objective of being happy; our lives are all different and yet the same.

—ANNE FRANK (1929-1945)
German/Dutch diarist

I've done more harm by the falseness of trying to please
than by the honesty of trying to hurt.

—JESSAMYN WEST (1907–1984)
American writer

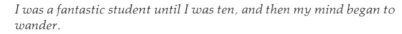

*I was a fantastic student until I was ten, and then my mind began to
wander.*

—GRACE PALEY, b. 1922
American writer

All loss is gain. Since I have become so near-sighted I see no dust or squalor, and therefore conceive of myself as living in splendor.

—ALICE JAMES (1848-1892)
American diarist

If you always do what interests you, then at least one person is pleased.

—Advice to Katharine Hepburn from her mother

Women are repeatedly accused of taking things personally. I cannot see any other honest way of taking them.

—MARYA MANNES (1904-1990)
American writer

I never hated a man enough to give him diamonds back.

—ZSA ZSA GABOR, b. 1923
Hungarian actress

Always there remains portions of our heart into which no one is able to enter, invite them as we may.

—MARY DIXON THAYER
20th-century American writer

Plain women know more about men than beautiful ones do.

—KATHARINE HEPBURN, b. 1909
American actress

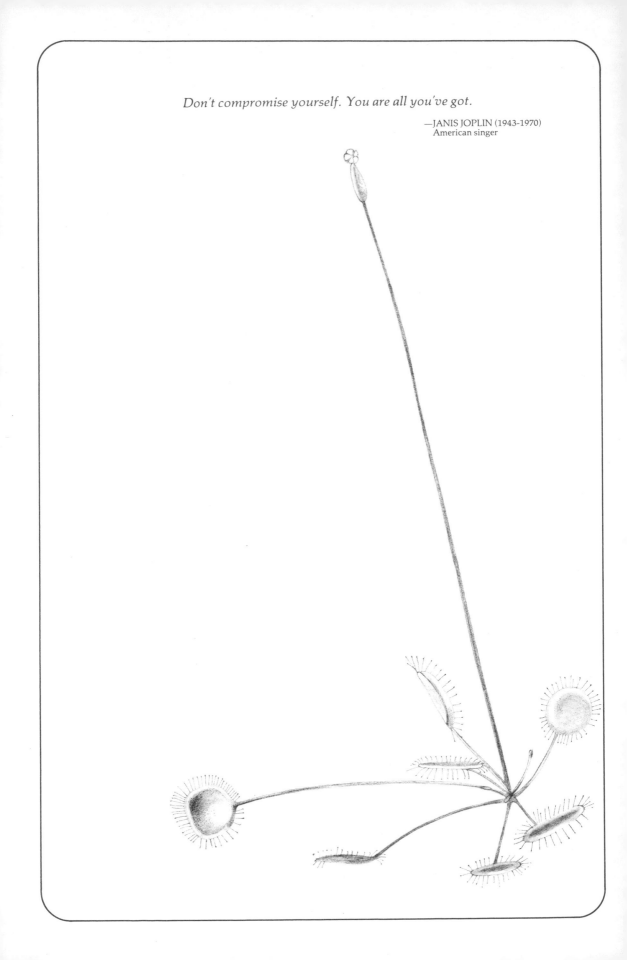

Don't compromise yourself. You are all you've got.

—JANIS JOPLIN (1943-1970)
American singer

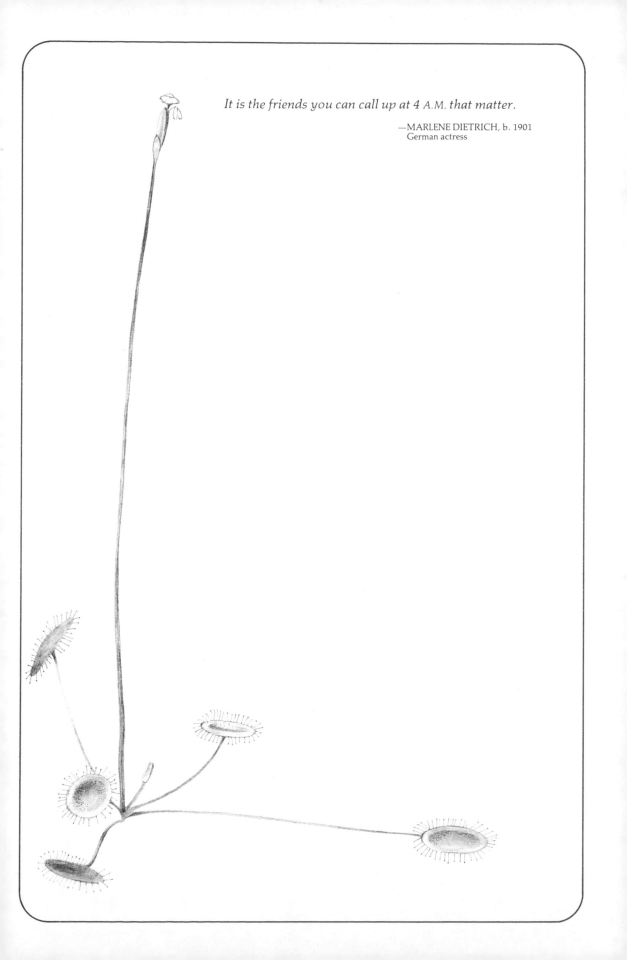

It is the friends you can call up at 4 A.M. that matter.

—MARLENE DIETRICH, b. 1901
German actress

The trouble with being in the rat race is that even if you win, you're still a rat.

—LILY TOMLIN, b. 1939
American actress & comedienne

It seemed to me that the desire to get married—which, I regret to say, I believe is basic and primal in women—is followed almost immediately by an equally basic and primal urge—which is to be single again.

—NORA EPHRON, b. 1941
American writer

I think it's the end of progress if you stand still and think of what you've done in the past. I keep on.

—LESLIE CARON, b.1931
French actress

Even cowards can endure hardship; only the brave can endure suspense.

—MIGNON McLAUGHLIN
American editor

A private railroad car is not an acquired taste. One takes to it immediately.

—ELEANOR R. (MRS. AUGUST) BELMONT (1879-1979)
English actress and philanthropist

What a lovely surprise to discover how un-lonely being alone can be.

—ELLEN BURSTYN, b. 1932
American actress

I don't wait for moods. You accomplish nothing if you do that. Your mind must know it has got to get down to earth.

—PEARL S. BUCK (1892-1973)
American writer & humanitarian

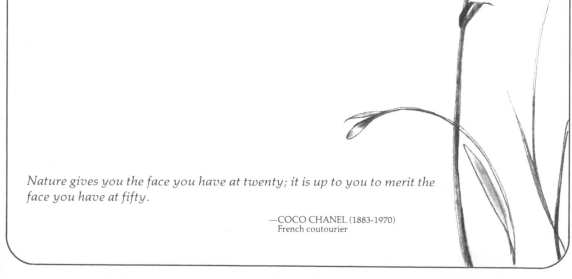

Nature gives you the face you have at twenty; it is up to you to merit the face you have at fifty.

—COCO CHANEL (1883-1970)
French coutourier

Life never becomes a habit to me. It's always a marvel.

—KATHERINE MANSFIELD (1888–1923)
New Zealand writer

Anger repressed can poison a relationship as surely as the cruelest words.

—DR. JOYCE BROTHERS, b. 1925
American psychologist

The especial genius of women I believe to be electrical in movement,
intuitive in function, spiritual in tendency.

—MARGARET FULLER (1810-1850)
American journalist

I'll walk where my own nature would be leading: It vexes me to choose another guide.

—EMILY BRONTË (1818-1848)
English novelist

Noble deeds and hot baths are the best cures for depression.

—DODIE SMITH, b. 1896
English playwright

There's a time when you have to explain to your children why they're born,
and it's a marvelous thing if you know the reason by then.

—HAZEL SCOTT, b. 1920
American/West Indian pianist

When a man gets up to speak, people listen then look. When a woman gets up, people look; *then, if they like what they see, they listen.*

—PAULINE FREDERICK (1883-1938)
American actress

To err is human—but it feels divine.

—MAE WEST (1893-1980)
American actress

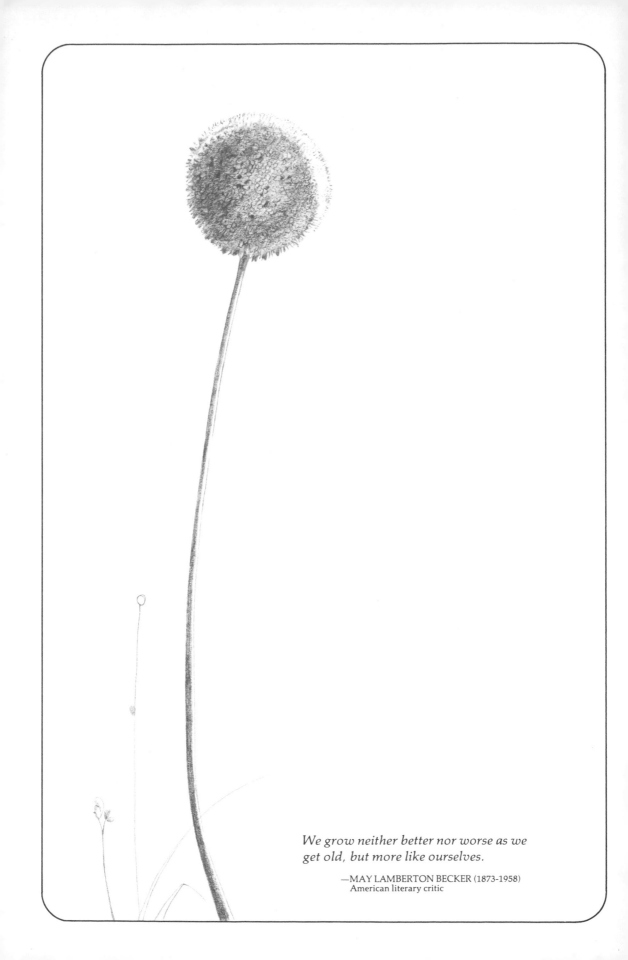

*We grow neither better nor worse as we
get old, but more like ourselves.*

—MAY LAMBERTON BECKER (1873-1958)
American literary critic

In real love you want the other person's good. In romantic love, you want the other person.

—MARGARET ANDERSON (1893-1973)
American publisher

No animal is so inexhaustible as an excited infant.

—AMY LESLIE (1860-1939)
American drama critic

If you have made mistakes . . . there is always another chance for you . . . you may have a fresh start any moment you choose, for this thing we call "failure" is not the falling down, but the staying down.

—MARY PICKFORD (1893-1979)
American actress

One of the oldest human needs is having someone to wonder where you are when you don't come home at night.

—MARGARET MEAD (1901-1978)
American cultural anthropologist

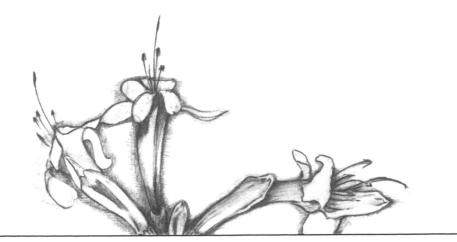

One thing life taught me—if you are interested, you never have to look for new interests. They come to you.

—ELEANOR ROOSEVELT (1884-1962)
American stateswoman & humanitarian

True enthusiasm is a fine feeling whose
flash I admire where-ever I see it.

—CHARLOTTE BRONTË (1816-1855)
English writer

You will do foolish things, but do them with enthusiasm.

—COLETTE (1873-1954)
French writer

And then, not expecting it, you become middle-aged and anonymous. No one notices you. You achieve a wonderful freedom. It is a positive thing. You can move about, unnoticed and invisible.

—DORIS LESSING, b. 1919
English writer

When he is late for dinner and I know he must be either having an affair or lying dead in the street, I always hope he's dead.

—JUDITH VIORST, b. 1931
American poet

Give me a dozen such heartbreaks, if that would help me lose a couple of pounds.

—COLETTE (1873-1954)
French writer

To be successful, the first thing to do is fall in love with your work.

—SISTER MARY LAURETTA
Roman Catholic Nun

. . . words are a form of action, capable of influencing change. Their articulation represents a complete, lived experience.

—INGRID BENGIS, b. 1944
American writer

Too much of a good thing can be wonderful.

—MAE WEST (1893-1980)
American actress

I know some good marriages—marriages where both people are just trying to get through their days by helping each other, being good to each other.

—ERICA JONG, b. 1942
American writer

Just remember, we're all in this alone.

—LILY TOMLIN, b. 1939
American actress & comedienne

Art is the only way to run away without leaving home.

—TWYLA THARP, b.1941
American choreographer

From birth to age 18 a girl needs good parents. From 18 to 35 she needs good looks. From 35 to 55 she needs a good personality. From 55 on, she needs good cash.

—SOPHIE TUCKER (1884-1966)
American singer

If you reach for something and find out it's the wrong thing, you change your program and go on.

—HAZEL SCOTT, b. 1920
West Indian/American pianist

We can do no great things—only small things with great love.

—MOTHER TERESA, b. 1910
Roman Catholic Missionary

I have a simple philosophy. Fill what's empty. Empty what's full. And scratch where it itches.

—ALICE ROOSEVELT LONGWORTH (1884-1980)
Daughter of Theodore Roosevelt

Mistakes are part of the dues one pays for a full life.

—SOPHIA LOREN, b. 1934
Italian actress

Love, like a chicken salad or restaurant hash, must be taken with blind faith or it loses its flavor.

—HELEN ROWLAND (1875-1950)
American writer

I think somehow we learn who we really are, then live with that decision.

—ELEANOR ROOSEVELT (1884-1962)
American stateswoman & humanitarian

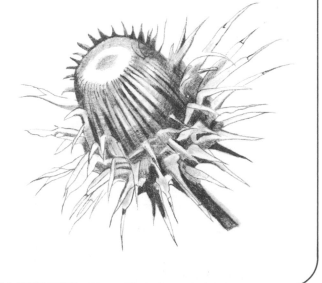

Life is what we make it, always has been, always will be.

—GRANDMA MOSES (1860-1961)
American primitive painter

We all live in suspense, from day to day, from hour to hour; in other words,
we are the hero of our own story.

—MARY McCARTHY (1912-1989)
American writer

Giving is the only flight in space permitted to human beings.

—ANAÏS NIN (1903-1977)
American/French writer

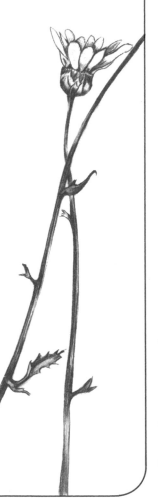

But to look back all the time is boring. Excitement lies in tomorrow.

—NATALIA MAKAROVA, b. 1940
Russian-American ballerina

To live is so startling it leaves little time for anything else.

—EMILY DICKINSON (1830-1886)
American poet

The basic discovery about any people is the discovery of the relationship between its men and women.

—PEARL S. BUCK (1892-1973)
American writer & humanitarian

The post office has a great charm at one point of our lives. When you have lived to my age, you will begin to think letters are never worth going through the rain for.

—JANE AUSTEN (1775-1815)
English novelist

You can't be brave if you've only had wonderful things happen to you.

—MARY TYLER MOORE, b. 1937
American actress

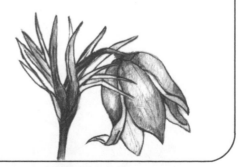

Time wounds all heels.

—JANE ACE (1905-1974)
American radio personality

Inside myself is a place where I live all alone, and that's where you renew your springs that never dry up.

—PEARL S. BUCK (1892-1973)
American writer & humanitarian

And the trouble is, if you don't risk anything, you risk even **more.**

—ERICA JONG, b. 1942
American writer

Well, being divorced is like being hit by a Mack truck. If you live through it, you start looking very carefully to the right and to the left.

—JEAN KERR, b. 1923
American playwright & humorist

Forgiveness is the key to action and freedom.

—HANNAH ARENDT (1906-1975)
German/American philosopher & historian

Whenever you want to marry someone, go have lunch with his ex-wife.

—SHELLEY WINTERS, b. 1922
American actress

Someone said that life is a party. You join in after it's started and leave before it's finished.

—ELSA MAXWELL
20th-century American socialite

I don't need a man to rectify my existence. The most profound relationship we'll ever have is the one with ourselves.

—SHIRLEY MacLAINE, b. 1934
American actress & dancer

The first problem for all of us, men and women, is not to learn, but to unlearn.

—GLORIA STEINEM, b. 1934
American feminist & writer

Who has words at the right moment?

—CHARLOTTE BRONTË (1816-1855)
English writer

The only thing that makes life possible is permanent, intolerable uncertainty; not knowing what comes next.

—URSULA K. LE GUIN, b. 1929
American writer

Superior people never make long visits.

—MARIANNE MOORE (1887–1972)
American poet

Time—our youth—it never really goes, does it? It is all held in our minds.

—HELEN HOOVEN SANTMYER
20th-century American writer

Think wrongly, if you please, but in all cases think for yourself.

—DORIS LESSING, b. 1919
English writer

It is terribly amusing how many different climates of feeling one can go through in one day.

—ANNE MORROW LINDBERGH, b. 1906
American writer & aviator

I am learning what I choose is the real me.

—ANONYMOUS

One of the many things nobody ever tells you about middle age is that it's such a nice change from being young.

—DOROTHY CANFIELD FISHER (1879-1958)
American writer

I always felt that the great high privilege, relief and comfort of friendship was that one had to explain nothing.

—KATHERINE MANSFIELD (1888–1923)
New Zealand writer

You must do the thing you think you cannot do.

—ELEANOR ROOSEVELT (1884-1962)
American stateswoman & humanitarian

Ideally, couples need three lives; one for him, one for her,
and one for them together.

—JACQUELINE BISSET, b. 1946
English actress

True feeling justifies whatever it may cost.

—MAY SARTON (1912–1985)
American writer

The giving of love is an education in itself.

—ELEANOR ROOSEVELT (1884-1962)
American stateswoman & humanitarian

I used to believe that anything was better than nothing. Now I know that sometimes nothing is better.

—GLENDA JACKSON, b. 1936
English actress

Hot fudge fills deep needs.

—SUSAN ISAACS
20th-century American writer

*Selfishness is not living as one wishes to live, it is
asking others to live as one wishes to live.*

—RUTH RENDELL, b. 1930
English writer

Cherish forever what makes you unique, 'cuz you're really a yawn if it goes!

—BETTE MIDLER, b. 1945
American entertainer

There is no pleasure in having nothing to do; the fun is in having lots to do and not doing it.

—MARY LITTLE, b. 1912
American writer & illustrator

There are many things in your heart you can never tell to another person.
They are you, your private joys and sorrows, and you can never tell them.
You cheapen them, the inside of yourself when you tell them.

—GRETA GARBO (1905–1990)
Swedish actress

It is sad to grow old but nice to ripen.

—BRIGITTE BARDOT, b.1934
French actress